CAMBRIDGE LIBRARY COLLECTION

Books of enduring scholarly value

Literary Studies

This series provides a high-quality selection of early printings of literary works, textual editions, anthologies and literary criticism which are of lasting scholarly interest. Ranging from Old English to Shakespeare to early twentieth-century work from around the world, these books offer a valuable resource for scholars in reception history, textual editing, and literary studies.

My Father as I Recall Him

The official biography of Charles Dickens (1812–70) was published in 1872–4 by his close friend and literary executor John Forster, and has been reissued in this series. Of the many other memoirs and reminiscences of the great novelist, this book by his favourite daughter Mary (1838–96), known as Mamie, is perhaps the least familiar. Published in 1896, shortly after her death, it gives a loving picture, based on her own memories, of the person whom she held 'in my heart of hearts as a man apart from all other men, as one apart from all other beings'. Mamie, who had taken Dickens's side during the separation from his wife, and acted effectively as his housekeeper at Gad's Hill, had compiled an edition of her father's letters with her aunt Georgina Hogarth, and this second act of piety gives an idyllic – perhaps too idyllic – account of daily life with Dickens.

Cambridge University Press has long been a pioneer in the reissuing of out-of-print titles from its own backlist, producing digital reprints of books that are still sought after by scholars and students but could not be reprinted economically using traditional technology. The Cambridge Library Collection extends this activity to a wider range of books which are still of importance to researchers and professionals, either for the source material they contain, or as landmarks in the history of their academic discipline.

Drawing from the world-renowned collections in the Cambridge University Library and other partner libraries, and guided by the advice of experts in each subject area, Cambridge University Press is using state-of-the-art scanning machines in its own Printing House to capture the content of each book selected for inclusion. The files are processed to give a consistently clear, crisp image, and the books finished to the high quality standard for which the Press is recognised around the world. The latest print-on-demand technology ensures that the books will remain available indefinitely, and that orders for single or multiple copies can quickly be supplied.

The Cambridge Library Collection brings back to life books of enduring scholarly value (including out-of-copyright works originally issued by other publishers) across a wide range of disciplines in the humanities and social sciences and in science and technology.

My Father
as I Recall Him

Mamie Dickens

CAMBRIDGE
UNIVERSITY PRESS

University Printing House, Cambridge, CB2 8BS, United Kingdom

Cambridge University Press is part of the University of Cambridge.
It furthers the University's mission by disseminating knowledge in the pursuit of
education, learning and research at the highest international levels of excellence.

www.cambridge.org
Information on this title: www.cambridge.org/9781108074551

© in this compilation Cambridge University Press 2014

This edition first published 1896
This digitally printed version 2014

ISBN 978-1-108-07455-1 Paperback

CHARLES DICKENS.

*MY FATHER AS
I RECALL HIM.*

The pages of this little book were in type and about to be sent for correction to my sister—who had been for some months in very delicate health—when she suddenly became still more gravely ill. The hand which had traced the words of love and veneration dedicated to our father's memory grew too feeble to hold a pen, and before the proofs of her little volume could be submitted to her for revision, my dear sister died.

K.P.

MAMIE DICKENS.

MY FATHER
AS I RECALL HIM.

BY

MAMIE DICKENS.

THE

ROXBURGHE PRESS,

FIFTEEN, VICTORIA STREET,

WESTMINSTER.

THIS WORK, AND ALL THE PUBLICATIONS OF THE ROXBURGHE PRESS, ARE SUPPLIED TO THE TRADE BY MESSRS. SIMPKIN, MARSHALL, HAMILTON, KENT & COMPANY, LIMITED, AND CAN BE OBTAINED THROUGH ANY BOOKSELLER.

CONTENTS.

CONTENTS—*continued.*

LIST OF ILLUSTRATIONS.

CHARLES DICKENS READING IN GARDEN.

My Father as I Recall Him.

CHAPTER I.

Seeing "Gad's Hill" as a child.—His domestic side and home-love.—His love of children.—His neatness and punctuality.—At the table, and as host.—The original of "Little Nell."

If, in these pages, written in remembrance of my father, I should tell you my dear friends, nothing new of him, I can, at least, promise you that what I shall tell will be told faithfully, if simply, and perhaps there may be some things not familiar to you.

A great many writers have taken it upon themselves to write lives of my father, to tell anecdotes of him, and to print all manner of things about him. Of all these published books I have read but one, the only genuine "Life" thus far written of him, the one sanctioned by my father himself,

namely: "The Life of Charles Dickens,'
by John Forster,

But in what I write about my father I
shall depend chiefly upon my own memory of
him, for I wish no other or dearer remembrance. My love for my father has never been
touched or approached by any other love.
I hold him in my heart of hearts as a man
apart from all other men, as one apart
from all other beings.

Of my father's childhood it is but natural
that I should know very little more than
the knowledge possessed by the great public.
But I never remember hearing him allude
at any time, or under any circumstances, to
those unhappy days in his life except in the
one instance of his childish love and admiration for "Gad's Hill," which was destined
to become so closely associated with his
name and works.

He had a very strong and faithful attachment for places: Chatham, I think, being
his first love in this respect. For it was

here, when a child, and a very sickly child,
poor little fellow, that he found in an old
spare room a store of books, among which
were "Roderick Random," "Peregrine
Pickle," "Humphrey Clinker," "Tom
Jones," "The Vicar of Wakefield," "Don
Quixote," "Gil Blas," "Robinson Crusoe,"
"The Arabian Nights," and other volumes.
"They were," as Mr. Forster wrote, "a
host of friends when he had no single
friend." And it was while living at Chatham
that he first saw "Gad's Hill."

As a "very queer small boy" he used to
walk up to the house—it stood on the
summit of a high hill—on holidays, or
when his heart ached for a "great treat."
He would stand and look at it, for as a
little fellow he had a wonderful liking and
admiration for the house, and it was, to
him, like no other house he had ever seen.
He would walk up and down before it with
his father, gazing at it with delight, and
the latter would tell him that perhaps if he

worked hard, was industrious, and grew up
to be a good man, he might some day
come to live in that very house. His love
for this place went through his whole life,
and was with him until his death. He takes
" Mr. Pickwick" and his friends from
Rochester to Cobham by the beautiful back
road, and I remember one day when we
were driving that way he showed me the
exact spot where " Mr. Winkle" called out:
" Whoa, I have dropped my whip!" After
his marriage he took his wife for the
honeymoon to a village called Chalk,
between Gravesend and Rochester.

Many years after, when he was living
with his family in a villa near Lausanne,
he wrote to a friend : " The green woods
and green shades about here are more like
Cobham, in Kent, than anything we dream
of at the foot of the Alpine passes." And
again, in still later years, one of his
favorite walks from " Gad's Hill" was to
a village called Shorne, where there was a

quaint old church and graveyard. He often said that he would like to be buried there, the peace and quiet of the homely little place having a tender fascination for him. So we see that his heart was always in Kent.

But let this single reference to his earlier years suffice, so that I may write of him during those years when I remember him among us and around us in our home.

From his earliest childhood, throughout his earliest married life to the day of his death, his nature was home-loving. He was a "home man" in every respect. When he became celebrated at a very early age, as we know, all his joys and sorrows were taken home; and he found there sympathy and the companionship of his "own familiar friends." In his letters to these latter, in his letters to my mother, to my aunt, and, later on, to us his children, he never forgot anything that he knew would be of interest about his work,

his successes, his hopes or fears. And
there was a sweet simplicity in his belief
that such news would most certainly be
acceptable to all, that is wonderfully touching and child-like coming from a man of
genius.

His care and thoughtfulness about home
matters, nothing being deemed too small or
trivial to claim his attention and consideration, were really marvellous when we remember his active, eager, restless, working
brain. No man was so inclined naturally to
derive his happiness from home affairs.
He was full of the kind of interest in a
house which is commonly confined to
women, and his care of and for us as wee
children did most certainly " pass the love
of women ! " His was a tender and most
affectionate nature.

For many consecutive summers we used
to be taken to Broadstairs. This little
place became a great favorite with my
father. He was always very happy there,

and delighted in wandering about the garden
of his house, generally accompanied by one
or other of his children. In later years, at
Boulogne, he would often have his youngest
boy, "The Noble Plorn," trotting by his side.
These two were constant companions in those
days, and after these walks my father
would always have some funny anecdote to
tell us. And when years later the time
came for the boy of his heart to go out
into the world, my father, after seeing him
off, wrote: "Poor Plorn has gone to
Australia. It was a hard parting at the
last. He seemed to become once more my
youngest and favorite little child as the
day drew near, and I did not think I
could have been so shaken. These are
hard, hard things, but they might have to
be done without means or influence, and
then they would be far harder. God bless
him!"

When my father was arranging and rehearsing his readings from "Dombey," the

death of "little Paul" caused him such
real anguish, the reading being so difficult
to him, that he told us he could only
master his intense emotion by keeping the
picture of Plorn, well, strong and hearty,
steadily before his eyes. We can see by
the different child characters in his books
what a wonderful knowledge he had of
children, and what a wonderful and truly
womanly sympathy he had with them in all
their childish joys and griefs. I can remember with us, his own children, how
kind, considerate and patient he always was.
But we were never afraid to go to him in
any trouble, and never had a snub from
him or a cross word under any circumstances. He was always glad to give us
"treats," as he called them, and used to
conceive all manner of those "treats" for
us, and if any favor had to be asked we
were always sure of a favorable answer.
On these occasions my sister "Katie" was
generally our messenger, we others waiting

outside the study door to hear the verdict. She and I used to have delightful treats in those summer evenings, driving up to Hampstead in the open carriage with him, our mother, and "Auntie," * and getting out for a long walk through the lovely country lanes, picking wild roses and other flowers, or walking hand in hand with him listening to some story.

There never existed, I think, in all the world, a more thoroughly tidy or methodical creature than was my father. He was tidy in every way—in his mind, in his handsome and graceful person, in his work, in keeping his writing table drawers, in his large correspondence, in fact in his whole life.

I remember that my sister and I occupied

* When I write about my aunt, or " Auntie," as no doubt I may often have occasion to do, it is of the aunt *par excellence*, Georgina Hogarth. She has been to me ever since I can remember anything, and to all of us, the truest, best and dearest friend, companion and counsellor. To quote my father's own words : "The best and truest friend man ever had."

a little garret room in Devonshire Terrace, at the very top of the house. He had taken the greatest pains and care to make the room as pretty and comfortable for his two little daughters as it could be made. He was often dragged up the steep stair-case to this room to see some new print or some new ornament which we children had put up, and he always gave us words of praise and approval. He encouraged us in every possible way to make ourselves useful, and to adorn and beautify our rooms with our own hands, and to be ever tidy and neat. I remember that the adornment of this garret was decidedly primitive, the unframed prints being fastened to the wall by ordinary black or white pins, whichever we could get. But, never mind, if they were put up neatly and tidily they were always "excellent," or "quite slap-up" as he used to say. Even in those early days, he made a point of visiting every room in the house once each morning, and if a

chair was out of its place, or a blind not
quite straight, or a crumb left on the floor,
woe betide the offender.

And then his punctuality! It was almost frightful to an unpunctual mind!
This again was another phase of his
extreme tidiness; it was also the outcome
of his excessive thoughtfulness and consideration for others. His sympathy, also,
with all pain and suffering made him quite
invaluable in a sick room. Quick, active,
sensible, bright and cheery, and sympathetic
to a degree, he would seize the "case" at
once, know exactly what to do and do it.
In all our childish ailments his visits were
eagerly looked forward to; and our little
hearts would beat a shade faster, and our
aches and pains become more bearable,
when the sound of his quick footstep was
heard, and the encouraging accents of his
voice greeted the invalid. I can remember
now, as if it were yesterday, how the touch
of his hand—he had a most sympathetic

B

touch—was almost too much sometimes, the help and hope in it making my heart full to overflowing. He believed firmly in the power of mesmerism, as a remedy in some forms of illness, and was himself a mesmerist of no mean order; I know of many cases, my own among the number, in which he used his power in this way with perfect success.

And however busy he might be, and even in his hours of relaxation, he was still, if you can understand me, always busy; he would give up any amount of time and spare himself no fatigue if he could in any way alleviate sickness and pain.

In very many of my father's books there are frequent references to delicious meals, wonderful dinners and more marvellous dishes, steaming bowls of punch, etc., which have led many to believe that he was a man very fond of the table. And yet I think no more abstemious man ever lived.

In the "Gad's Hill" days, when the
house was full of visitors, he had a peculiar
notion of always having the menu for the
day's dinner placed on the sideboard at
luncheon time. And then he would discuss
every item in his fanciful, humorous way
with his guests, much to this effect:
" Cock-a-leekie? Good, decidedly good;
fried soles with shrimp sauce? Good
again; croquettes of chicken? Weak,
very weak; decided want of imagination
here," and so on, and he would apparently
be so taken up with the merits or demerits
of a menu that one might imagine he lived
for nothing but the coming dinner. He
had a small but healthy appetite, but was
remarkably abstemious both in eating and
drinking.

He was delightful as a host, caring
individually for each guest, and bringing
the special qualities of each into full notice
and prominence, putting the very shyest
at his or her ease, making the best of the

most humdrum, and never thrusting himself forward.

But when he was most delightful, was
alone with us at home and sitting over
dessert, and when my sister was with us
especially—I am talking now of our grown-
up days—for she had great power in
"drawing him out." At such times although
he might sit down to dinner in a grave or
abstracted mood, he would, invariably, soon
throw aside his silence and end by delight-
ing us all with his genial talk and his quaint
fancies about people and things. He was
always, as I have said, much interested
in mesmerism, and the curious influence exer-
cised by one personality over another. One
illustration I remember his using was, that
meeting someone in the busy London streets,
he was on the point of turning back to accost
the supposed friend, when finding out his
mistake in time he walked on again until he actually met the real friend, whose shadow, as it

were, but a moment ago had come across his path.

And then the forgetting of a word or a name. "Now into what pigeon-hole of my brain did that go, and why do I suddenly remember it now?" And as these thoughts passed through his mind and were spoken dreamily, so they also appeared in his face. Another instant, perhaps, and his eyes would be full of fun and laughter.

At the beginning of his literary career he suffered a great sorrow in the death—a very sudden death—of my mother's sister, Mary Hogarth. She was of a most charming and lovable disposition, as well as being personally very beautiful. Soon after my parents married, Aunt Mary was constantly with them. As her nature developed she became my father's ideal of what a young girl should be. And his own words show how this great affection and the influence of the girl's loved memory were with him to the end of his life. The shock of her sudden death so affected and prostrated him that the publication of "Pickwick" was interrupted for two months.

"I look back," he wrote, "and with unmingled pleasure, to every link which each ensuing week has added to the chain of our attachment. It shall go hard I hope ere anything but death impairs the toughness of a bond now so firmly riveted. That beautiful passage you were so kind and considerate as to send to me has given me the only feeling akin to pleasure, sorrowful pleasure it is, that I have yet had connected with the loss of my dear young friend and companion, for whom my love and attachment will never diminish, and by whose side, if it please God to leave me in possession of sense to signify my wishes, my bones whenever or wherever I die, will one day be laid."

She was buried in Kensal Green Cemetery, and her grave bears the following inscription, written by my father:

"Young, beautiful, and good, God in His mercy numbered her among His angels at the early age of seventeen."

A year after her death, in writing to my mother from Yorkshire, he says: "Is it not extraordinary that the same dreams which have constantly visited me since poor Mary died follow me everywhere? After all the change of scene and fatigue I have dreamt of her ever since I left home, and no doubt shall until I return. I would fain believe, sometimes, that her spirit may have some influence over them, but their perpetual repetition is extraordinary."

In the course of years there came changes in our home, inevitable changes. But no changes could ever alter my father's home-loving nature. As he wrote to Mr. Forster, as a young man, so it was with him to the time of his death: "We

shall soon meet, please God, and be
happier than ever we were in all our lives.
Oh ! home—home—home ! ! !

A CHRISTMAS CARD, BY AN UNKNOWN ARTIST, SENT TO CHARLES DICKENS.

CHAPTER II.

Christmas was always a time which in our home was looked forward to with eagerness and delight, and to my father it was a time dearer than any other part of the year, I think. He loved Christmas for its deep significance as well as for its joys, and this he demonstrates in every allusion in his writings to the great festival, a day which he considered should be fragrant with the love that we should bear one to another, and with the love and reverence of his Saviour and Master. Even in his most merry conceits of Christmas, there are always subtle and tender touches which will bring tears to the eyes, and make even the thoughtless have some special veneration for this most blessed anniversary.

In our childish days my father used to take us, every twenty-fourth day of December, to a toy shop in Holborn, where we were allowed to select our Christmas presents, and also any that we wished to give to our little companions. Although I believe we were often an hour or more in the shop before our several tastes were satisfied, he never showed the least impatience, was always interested, and as desirous as we, that we should choose exactly what we liked best. As we grew older, present giving was confined to our several birthdays, and this annual visit to the Holborn toy shop ceased.

When we were only babies my father determined that we should be taught to dance, so as early as the Genoa days we were given our first lessons. "Our oldest boy and his sisters are to be waited upon next week by a professor of the noble art of dancing," he wrote to a friend at this time. And again, in writing to my mother, he says: "I hope the dancing lessons will be a success. Don't fail to let me know."

Our progress in the graceful art delighted him, and his admiration of our success was evident when we exhibited to him, as we were perfected in them, all the steps, exercises and dances which formed our lessons. He always encouraged us in our dancing, and praised our grace and aptness, although criticized quite severely in some places for allowing his children to expend so much time and energy upon the training of their feet.

When "the boys" came home for the holidays there were constant rehearsals for the Christmas and New Year's parties; and more especially for the dance on Twelfth Night, the anniversary of my brother Charlie's birthday. Just before one of these celebrations my father insisted that my sister Katie and I should teach the polka step to Mr. Leech and himself My

father was as much in earnest about learning to take that wonderful step correctly,
as though there were nothing ot greater
importance in the world. Often he would
practice gravely in a corner, without either
partner or music, and I remember one cold
winter's night his awakening with the fear
that he had forgotten the step so strong
upon him that, jumping out of bed, by the
scant illumination of the old-fashioned
rushlight, and to his own whistling, he
diligently rehearsed its " one, two, three, one,
two, three" until he was once more secure
in his knowledge.

No one can imagine our excitement and
nervousness when the evening came on
which we were to dance with our pupils.
Katie, who was a very little girl was to
have Mr. Leech, who was over six feet
tall, for her partner, while my father was
to be mine. My heart beat so fast
that I could scarcely breathe, I was so
fearful for the success of our exhibition.

MR. JOHN LEECH.

But my fears were groundless, and we were greeted at the finish of our dance with hearty applause, which was more than compensation for the work which had been expended upon its learning.

My father was certainly not what in the ordinary acceptation of the term would be called " a good dancer." I doubt whether he had ever received any instruction in "the noble art" other than that which my sister and I gave him. In later years I remember trying to teach him the Schottische, a dance which he particularly admired and desired to learn. But although he was so fond of dancing, except at family gatherings in his own or his most intimate friends' homes, I never remember seeing him join in it himself, and I doubt if, even as a young man, he ever went to balls. Graceful in motion, his dancing, such as it was, was natural to him. Dance music was delightful to his cheery, genial spirit; the time and steps of a dance suited his tidy

nature, if I may so speak.   The action
and the exercise seemed to be a part of his
abundant vitality.

While I am writing of my father's fondness for dancing, a characteristic anecdote
of him occurs to me.   While he was court-
ing my mother, he went one summer
evening to call upon her.   The Hogarths
were living a little way out of London, in
a residence which had a drawing-room
opening with French windows on to a
lawn.   In this room my mother and her
family were seated quietly after dinner on
this particular evening, when suddenly a
young sailor jumped through one of the
open windows into the apartment, whistled
and danced a hornpipe, and before they
could recover from their amazement jumped
out again.   A few minutes later my father
walked in at the door as sedately as though
quite innocent of the prank, and shook
hands with everyone; but the sight of
their amazed faces proving too much for

his attempted sobriety, his hearty laugh was the signal for the rest of the party to join in his merriment. But judging from his slight ability in later years, I fancy that he must have taken many lessons to secure his perfection in that hornpipe.

His dancing was at its best, I think, in the "Sir Roger de Coverly"—and in what are known as country dances. In the former, while the end couples are dancing, and the side couples are supposed to be still, my father would insist upon the sides keeping up a kind of jig step, and clapping his hands to add to the fun, and dancing at the backs of those whose enthusiasm he thought needed rousing, was himself never still for a moment until the dance was over. He was very fond of a country dance which he learned at the house of some dear friends at Rockingham Castle, which began with quite a stately minuet to the tune of "God save the Queen, and then dashed suddenly

into "Down the Middle and up Again.
His enthusiasm in this dance, I remember,
was so great that, one evening after some
of our Tavistock House theatricals, when I
was thoroughly worn out with fatigue, being
selected by him as his partner, I caught
the infection of his merriment, and my
weariness vanished. As he himself says, in
describing dear old "Fezziwig's" Christmas
party, we were "people who would dance
and had no notion of walking." His enjoyment of all our frolics was equally keen,
and he writes to an American friend,
à propos of one of our Christmas merry-
makings: "Forster is out again; and if he
don't go in again after the manner in which
we have been keeping Christmas, he must
be very strong indeed. Such dinings, such
conjurings, such blindman's buffings, such
theatre goings, such kissings out of old
years and kissings in of new ones never
took place in these parts before. To keep
the Chuzzlewit going, and to do this little

book, the Carol, in the odd times between
two parts of it, was, as you may suppose,
pretty tight work. But when it was done
I broke out like a madman, and if you
could have seen me at a children's party at
Macready's the other night going down a
country dance with Mrs. M. you would
have thought I was a country gentleman
of independent property residing on a tip-
top farm, with the wind blowing straight
in my face every day."

At our holiday frolics he used sometimes
to conjure for us, the equally "noble art"
of the prestidigitateur being among his
accomplishments. He writes of this, which
he included in the list of our Twelfth Night
amusements, to another American friend:
" The actuary of the national debt couldn't
calculate the number of children who are
coming here on Twelfth Night, in honor
of Charlie's birthday, for which occasion I
have provided a magic lantern and divers
other tremendous engines of that nature.

But the best of it is that Forster and I have purchased between us the entire stock-in-trade of a conjuror, the practice and display whereof is entrusted to me. And if you could see me conjuring the company's watches into impossible tea-caddies and causing pieces of money to fly, and burning pocket handkerchiefs without burning 'em, and practising in my own room without anybody to admire, you would never forget it as long as you live."

One of these conjuring tricks comprised the disappearance and reappearance of a tiny doll, which would announce most unexpected pieces of news and messages to the different children in the audience ; this doll was a particular favorite, and its arrival eagerly awaited and welcomed.

That he loved to emphasize Christmas in every possible way, the following extract from a note which he sent me in December, 1868, will evidence. After speaking of a reading which he was to give on Christmas

Eve, he says : " It occurs to me that my table at St. James' Hall might be appropriately ornamented with a little holly next Tuesday. If the two front legs were entwined with it, for instance, and a border of it ran round the top of the fringe in front, with a little sprig by way of bouquet at each corner, it would present a seasonable appearance. If you think of this and will have the materials ready in a little basket, I will call for you at the office and take you up to the hall where the table will be ready for you."

But I think that our Christmas and New Year's tides at "Gad's Hill" were the happiest of all. Our house was always filled with guests, while a cottage in the village was reserved for the use of the bachelor members of our holiday party. My father himself, always deserted work for the week, and that was almost our greatest treat. He was the fun and life of those gatherings, the true Christmas spirit of

sweetness and hospitality filling his large
and generous heart. Long walks with him
were daily treats to be remembered. Games
passed our evenings merrily. "Proverbs,"
a game of memory, was very popular, and
it was one in which either my aunt or
myself was apt to prove winner. Father's
annoyance at our failure sometimes was
very amusing, but quite genuine. "Dumb
Crambo" was another favorite, and one in
which my father's great imitative ability
showed finely. I remember one evening
his dumb showing of the word "frog"
was so extremely laughable that the
memory of it convulsed Marcus Stone,
the clever artist, when he tried some time
later to imitate it.

One very severe Christmas, when the
snow was so deep as to make out-door
amusement or entertainment for our guests
impossible, my father suggested that he
and the inhabitants of the "bachelors'
cottage" should pass the time in unpack-

ing the French chalet, which had been
sent to him by Mr. Fetcher, and which
reached Higham Station in a large number
of packing cases. Unpacking these and
fitting the pieces together gave them
interesting employment, and some topics
of conversation for our luncheon party.

Our Christmas Day dinners at "Gad's
Hill" were particularly bright and cheery,
some of our nearest neighbours joining our
home party. The Christmas plum pudding had its own special dish of coloured
"repoussé" china, ornamented with holly.
The pudding was placed on this with a
sprig of real holly in the centre, lighted,
and in this state placed in front of my
father, its arrival being always the signal
for applause. A prettily decorated table
was his special pleasure, and from my
earliest girlhood the care of this devolved
upon me. When I had everything in
readiness, he would come with me to
inspect the result of my labors, before dress-

ing for dinner, and no word except of praise ever came to my ears.

He was a wonderfully neat and rapid carver, and I am happy to say taught me some of his skill in this. I used to help him in our home parties at " Gad's Hill " by carving at a side table, returning to my seat opposite him as soon as my duty was ended. On Christmas Day we all had our glasses filled, and then my father, raising his, would say: " Here's to us all. God bless us!" a toast which was rapidly and willingly drunk. His conversation, as may be imagined, was often extremely humorous, and I have seen the servants, who were waiting at table, convulsed often with laughter at his droll remarks and stories. Now, as I recall these gatherings, my sight grows blurred with the tears that rise to my eyes. But I love to remember them, and to see, if only in memory, my father at his own table, surrounded by

his own family and friends—a beautiful
Christmas spirit.

"It is good to be children sometimes,
and never better than at Christmas, when
its Mighty Founder was a child himself,"
was his own advice, and advice which he
followed both in letter and spirit.

One morning—it was the last day of the
year, I remember—while we were at breakfast at "Gad's Hill," my father suggested
that we should celebrate the evening by a
charade to be acted in pantomime. The
suggestion was received with acclamation,
and amid shouts and laughing we were
then and there, guests and members of the
family, allotted our respective parts. My
father went about collecting "stage proper-
ties," rehearsals were "called" at least
four times during the morning, and in all
our excitement no thought was given to
that necessary part of a charade, the
audience, whose business it is to guess the
pantomime. At luncheon someone asked

suddenly: " But what about an audience?"
"Why, bless my soul," said my father, "I'd
forgotten all about that." Invitations were
quickly dispatched to our neighbours, and
additional preparations made for supper.
In due time the audience came, and the
charade was acted so successfully that the
evening stands out in my memory as one
of the merriest and happiest of the many
merry and happy evenings in our dear old
home. My father was so extremely funny
in his part that the rest of us found it
almost impossible to maintain sufficient
control over ourselves to enable the charade
to proceed as it was planned to do.
It wound up with a country dance, which
had been invented that morning and practised quite a dozen times through the day,
and which was concluded at just a few
moments before midnight. Then leading
us all, characters and audience, out into
the wide hall, and throwing wide open the
door, my father, watch in hand, stood

waiting to hear the bells ring in the New Year. All was hush and silence after the laughter and merriment! Suddenly the peal of bells sounded, and turning he said: "A happy New Year to us all! God bless us." Kisses, good wishes and shaking of hands brought us again back to the fun and gaiety of a few moments earlier. Supper was served, the hot mulled wine drunk in toasts, and the maddest and wildest of "Sir Roger de Coverlys" ended our evening and began our New Year.

One New year's day my father organized some field sports in a meadow which was at the back of our house. "Foot races for the villagers come off in my field tomorrow," he wrote to a friend, "and we have been hard at work all day, building a course, making countless flags, and I don't know what else, Layard (the late Sir Henry Layard) is chief commissioner of the domestic police. The country police predict an immense crowd."

There were between two and three thousand people present at these sports, and by a kind of magical influence, my father seemed to rule every creature present to do his or her best to maintain order. The likelihood of things going wrong was anticipated, and despite the general prejudice of the neighbours against the undertaking, my father's belief and trust in his guests was not disappointed. But you shall have his own account of his success. "We had made a very pretty course," he wrote, and taken great pains. Encouraged by the cricket matches' experience, I allowed the landlord of the Falstaff to have a drinking booth on the ground. Not to seem to dictate or distrust, I gave all the prizes in money. The great mass of the crowd were laboring men of all kinds, soldiers, sailors and navvies. They did not, between half-past ten, when we began, and sunset, displace a rope or a stake; and they left every barrier and flag as neat as they found it.

There was not a dispute, and there was no drunkenness whatever. I made them a little speech from the lawn at the end of the games, saying that, please God, we would do it again next year. They cheered most lustily and dispersed. The road between this and Chatham was like a fair all day; and surely it is a fine thing to get such perfect behaviour out of a reckless seaport town." He was the last to realize, I am sure that it was his own sympathetic nature which gave him the love and honor of all classes, and that helped to make the day's sports such a great success!

My father was again in his element at the Twelfth Night parties to which I have before alluded. For many consecutive years, Miss Coutts, now the Baroness Burdett Coutts, was in the habit of sending my brother, on this his birthday anniversary, the most gorgeous of Twelfth-cakes, with an accompanying box of bon-bons and Twelfth Night characters. The

cake was cut, and the favors and bonbons
distributed at the birthday supper, and it
was then that my father's kindly, genial
nature overflowed in merriment. He would
have something droll to say to everyone,
and under his attentions the shyest child
would brighten and become merry. No one
was overlooked or forgotten by him; like
the young Cratchits, he was "ubiquitous."
Supper was followed by songs and recita-
tions from the various members of the
company, my father acting always as
master of ceremonies, and calling upon first
one child, then another for his or her con-
tribution to the festivity. I can see now
the anxious faces turned toward the beam-
ing, laughing eyes of their host. How
attentively he would listen, with his head
thrown slightly back, and a little to one
side, a happy smile on his lips. O, those
merry, happy times, never to be forgotten
by any of his own children, or by any of
their guests. Those merry, happy times!

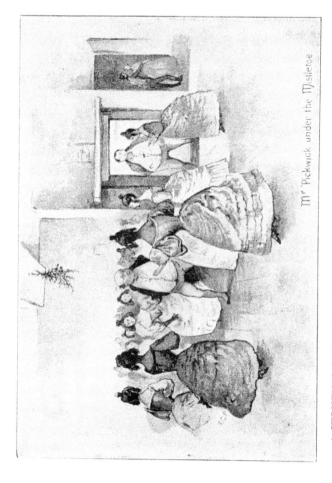

Mr Pickwick under the Mistletoe

A CHRISTMAS CARD, BY AN UNKNOWN ARTIST, SENT TO CHARLES DICKENS.

And in writing thus of these dear old holidays, when we were all so happy in our home, and when my father was with us, let me add this little postscript, and greet you on this Christmas of 1896, with my father's own words: " Reflect upon your present blessings—of which every man has many—not on your past misfortunes, of which all men have some. Fill your glass again with a merry face and contented heart. Our life on it, but your Christmas shall be merry and your New Year a happy one.

" So may the New Year be a happy one to you, happy to many more whose happiness depends on you! So may each year be happier than the last, and not the meanest of our brethren or sisterhood debarred their rightful share in what our great Creator formed them to enjoy."

CHAPTER III.

My father at his work.—Rooms in which he wrote.—Love
for his child characters.—Genius for character drawing.—
Nicholas Nickleby.—His writing hours.—His only
amanuensis.—"Pickwick" and "Boz."—Death of Mr.
Thackeray.

When at work my father was almost
always alone, so that, with rare exceptions,
save as we could see the effect of the
adventures of his characters upon him in
his daily moods, we knew but little of
his manner of work. Absolute quiet
under these circumstances was essential,
the slightest sound making an interrup-
tion fatal to the success of his labors,
although, oddly enough, in his leisure
hours the bustle and noise of a great
city seemed necessary to him. He writes,
after an enforced idleness of two years,
spent in a quiet place; "The difficulty of
going at what I call a rapid pace is

prodigious; indeed, it is almost an impossibility. I suppose this is partly the effect of two years' ease, and partly the absence of streets, and numbers of figures. I cannot express how much I want these. It seems as if they supplied something to my brain which, when busy, it cannot bear to lose. For a week or fortnight I can write prodigiously in a retired place, a day in London setting and starting me up again. But the toil and labor of writing day after day without that magic lantern is immense !"

As I have said, he was usually alone when at work, though there were, of course, some occasional exceptions, and I myself constituted such an exception. During our life at Tavistock House, I had a long and serious illness, with an almost equally long convalescence. During the latter, my father suggested that I should be carried every day into his study to remain with him, and, although I was fearful of disturbing him, he assured me that he desired to have me

with him.   On one of these mornings, I
was lying on the sofa endeavouring to keep
perfectly quiet, while my father wrote busily
and rapidly at his desk, when he suddenly
jumped from his chair and rushed to a
mirror which hung near, and in which I could
see the reflection of some extraordinary
facial contortions which he was making.
He returned rapidly to his desk, wrote
furiously for a few moments, and then went
again to the mirror.   The facial pantomime
was resumed, and then turning toward, but
evidently not seeing, me, he began talking
rapidly in a low voice.   Ceasing this soon,
however, he returned once more to his desk,
where he remained silently writing until
luncheon time.   It was a most curious
experience for me, and one of which, I did
not until later years, fully appreciate the
purport.   Then I knew that with his natural
intensity he had thrown himself completely
into the character that he was creating, and
that for the time being he had not only lost

sight of his surroundings, but had actually become in action, as in imagination, the creature of his pen.

His " studies " were always cheery, pleasant rooms, and always, like himself, the personification of neatness and tidiness. On the shelf of his writing table were many dainty and useful ornaments, gifts from his friends or members of his family, and always, a vase of bright and fresh flowers. The first study that I remember is the one in our Devonshire Terrace home, a pretty room, with steps leading directly into the garden from it, and with an extra baize door to keep out all sounds and noise. The study at Tavistock House was more elaborate ; a fine large room, opening into the drawing-room by means of sliding doors. When the rooms were thrown together they gave my father a promenade of considerable length for the constant indoor walking which formed a favorite recreation for him after a hard day's writing.

D

At "Gad's Hill" he first made a study
from one of the large spare sleeping rooms
of the house, as the windows there overlooked a beautiful and favorite view of his.
His writing table was always placed near a
window looking out into the open world
which he loved so keenly.   Afterwards he
occupied for years a smaller room over-
looking the back garden and a pretty
meadow, but this he eventually turned into
a miniature billiard room, and then
established himself, finally, in the room on
the right side of the entrance hall facing
the front garden.   It is this room which
Mr. Luke Fildes, the great artist and
our own esteemed friend, made famous
in his picture "The Empty Chair," which
he sketched for "The Graphic" after my
father's death.   The writing table, the
ornaments, the huge waste paper basket,
which "the master" had made for his own
use, are all there, and, alas, the empty chair!
That he was always in earnest, that he

lived with his creations, that their joys and sorrows were his joys and sorrows, that at times his anguish, both of body and spirit, was poignant and heart-breaking, I know. His interest in and love for his characters were intense as his nature, and is shown nowhere more strongly than in his sufferings during his portrayal of the short life of "Little Nell," like a father he mourned for his little girl—the child of his brain—and he writes: "I am, for the time, nearly dead with work and grief for the loss of my child." Again he writes of her: "You can't imagine (gravely I write and speak) how exhausted I am to-day with yesterday's labors. I went to bed last night utterly dispirited and done up. All night I have been pursued by the child; and this morning I am unrefreshed and miserable. I do not know what to do with myself."

His love and care for this little one are

shown most pathetically in the suggestions
which he gave to Mr. George Cattermole for
his illustrations of the "Old Curiosity Shop."
" Kit, the single gentleman, and Mr.
Garland go down to the place where the
child is and arrive there at night.   There
has been a fall of snow.   Kit, leaving them
behind, runs to the old house, and with a
lantern in one hand, and the bird in its cage
in the other, stops for a moment at a little
distance, with a natural hesitation, before he
goes up to make his presence known.   In a
window—supposed to be that of the child's
little room—a light is burning, and in that
room the child (unknown, of course, to her
visitors, who are full of hope), lies dead."

Again : " The child lying dead in the little
sleeping room, behind the open screen.
It is winter time, so there are no flowers,
but upon her breast and pillow there may
be strips of holly and berries and such green
things.   A window, overgrown with ivy.
The little boy who had that talk with her

about the angels may be by the bedside, if
you like it so; but I think it will be quieter
and more peaceful if she is quite alone. I
want the scene to express the most beautiful
repose and tranquillity, and to have something of a happy look, if death can do this."

Another: "The child has been buried
within the church, and the old man, who
cannot be made to understand that she is
dead repairs to the grave and sits there all
day long, waiting for her arrival to begin
another journey. His staff and knapsack,
her little bonnet and basket, lie beside him.
'She'll come to-morrow,' he says, when it
gets dark, and then goes sorrowfully home.
I think an hour glass running out would
keep up the notion; perhaps her little things
upon his knee or in his hand. I am break-
ing my heart over this story, and cannot
bear to finish it."

In acknowledging the receipt of a letter
concerning this book from Mr. John Tomlin,
an American, he wrote: "I thank you

cordially and heartily for your letter, and
for its kind and courteous terms. To think
that I have awakened among the vast
solitudes in which you dwell a fellow feeling
and sympathy with the creatures of many
thoughtful hours, is the source of the purest
delight and pride to me ; and believe me that
your expressions of affectionate remembrance
and approval, sounding from the green
forests of the Mississippi, sink deeper into
my heart and gratify it more than all the
honorary distinctions that all the courts of
Europe could confer. It is such things as
these that make one hope one does not live
in vain, and that are the highest rewards of
an author's life."

His genius for character sketching needs
no proof—his characters live to vouch for
themselves, for their reality. It is ever
amazing to me that the hand which drew
the pathetic and beautiful creations, the
kindly humored men, the lovely women, the
unfortunate little ones, could portray also

with such marvellous accuracy the villainy
and craftiness of such characters as Bumble,
Bill Sykes, Pecksniff, Uriah Heep and
Squeers. Undoubtedly from his earliest
childhood he had possessed the quick per-
ception, the instinct, which could read in
people's characters their tendencies toward
good and evil, and throughout his life he
valued this ability above literary skill and
finish. Mr. Forster makes a point of this
in his biography, speaking of the noticeable
traits in him: "What I had most, indeed,
to notice in him at the very outset of his
career, was his indifference to any praise of
his performances on their merely literary
merit, compared with the higher recognition
of them as bits of actual life, with the
meaning and purpose on their part, and the
responsibility on his, of realities rather than
creatures of fancy."

But he was always pleased with praise,
and always modest and grateful in returning
it. "How can I thank you?" he writes to

a friend who was expressing his pleasure at
" Oliver Twist."   " Can I do better than by
saying that the sense of poor Oliver's reality,
which I know you have had from the first,
has been the highest of all praise to me?
None that has been lavished upon me have
I felt half so much as that appreciation of
my intent and meaning.   Your notices make
me very grateful, but very proud, so have a
care."

The impressions which were later con-
verted into motives and plots for his stories
he imbibed often in his earliest childhood.
The crusade against the Yorkshire schools
which is waged in "Nicholas Nickleby," is
the working out of some of these childish
impressions.   He writes himself of them :
" I cannot call to mind how I came to hear
about Yorkshire schools, when I was not a
very robust child, sitting in by-places near
Rochester Castle with a head full of
Partridge, Strap, Tom Pipes and Sancho
Panza, but I know my first impressions of

the schools were picked up at this time."
We can imagine how deeply the wrongs
must have sunk into the sensitive heart of
of the child, rankling there through many
years, to bear fruit in the scourging of them
and their abuses from the land. While he
was at work upon "Nicholas Nickleby," he
sent one of his characteristic letters in reply
to a little boy—Master Hasting Hughes—
who wrote to ask him to make some
changes in the story. As some of you may
not have read this letter, and as it is so
extremely amusing, I shall quote part of it:

" DOUGHTY STREET, LONDON.
" December 12th, 1838.
" Respected Sir: I have given Squeers
one cut on the neck, and two on the head,
at which he appeared much surprised, and
began to cry, which, being a cowardly thing,
is just what I should have expected from
him—wouldn't you?
" I have carefully done what you told me
in your letter about the lamb and the two

'sheeps' for the little boys. They have also
had some good ale and porter and some
wine. I am sorry you did not say what wine
you would like them to have. I gave them
some sherry, which they liked very much,
except one boy who was a little sick and
choked a good deal. He was rather greedy,
and that's the truth, and I believe it went
the wrong way, which I say served him,
right, and I hope you will say so too. Nick
has had his roast lamb, as you said he was
to, but he could not eat it all, and says if
you do not mind his doing so he should like
to have the rest hashed to-morrow with
some greens, which he is very fond of, and
so am I. He said he did not like to have
his porter hot, for he thought it spoilt the
flavour, so I let him have it cold. You
should have seen him drink it. I thought
he never would have left off. I also gave
him three pounds in money, all in sixpences
to make it seem more, and he said directly
that he should give more than half to his

mamma and sister, and divide the rest with
poor Smike. And I say he is a good fellow
for saying so ; and if anybody says he isn't,
I am ready to fight him whenever they like
—there!

"Fanny Squeers shall be attended to,
depend upon it. Your drawing of her is
very like, except that I do not think the
hair is quite curly enough. The nose is
particularly like hers, and so are the legs.
She is a nasty, disagreeable thing, and I
know it will make her very cross when she
sees it, and what I say is that I hope it
may. You will say the same, I know—at
least I think you will."

The amount of work which he could
accomplish varied greatly at certain times,
though in its entirety it was so immense.
When he became the man of letters, and
ceased the irregular, unmethodical life of
the reporter, his mornings were invariably
spent at his desk. The time between breakfast and luncheon, with an occasional

extension of a couple of hours into the afternoon, were given over to his creations. The exceptions were when he was taking a holiday or resting, though even when ostensibly employed in the latter, cessation from story writing meant the answering of letters and the closer attention to his business matters, so that but little of real rest ever came into his later life.

While in Italy he gave a fragmentary diary of his daily life in a letter to a friend, and the routine was there very much what it was at home. "I am in a regular ferocious excitement with the Chimes; get up at seven; have a cold bath before breakfast; and blaze away, wrathful and red-hot, until three o'clock or so, when I usually knock off (unless it rains) for the day. I am fierce to finish in a spirit bearing some affinity to that of truth and mercy, and to shame the cruel and the wicked, but it is hard work." His entire discomfort under sound interruptions is also shown in the above, in his reference to the Chimes, and the effect which they had upon him.

Despite his regularity of working hours, as I have said, the amount of work which my father accomplished varied greatly. His manuscripts were usually written upon white "slips," though sometimes upon blue paper, and there were many mornings when it would be impossible for him to fill one of these. He writes on one occasion : " I am sitting at home, patiently waiting for Oliver Twist, who has not yet arrived." And, indeed, " Oliver" gave him considerable trouble, in the course of his adventures, by his disinclination to be put upon paper easily. This slowness in writing marked more prominently the earlier period of my father's literary career, though these " blank days," when his brain refused to work, were of occasional occurrence to the end. He was very critical of his own labors, and would bring nothing but the best of his brain to the art which he so dearly loved

—his venerated mistress. But, on the other hand, the amount of work which he would accomplish at other times was almost incredible. During a long sojourn at Lausanne he writes: " I have not been idle since I have been here. I had a good deal to write for Lord John about the ragged schools; so I set to work and did that. A good deal to Miss Coutts, in reference to her charitable projects; so I set to work and did that. Half of the children's New Testament to write, or pretty nearly. I set to work and did that. Next, I cleared off the greater part of such correspondence as I had rashly pledged myself to, and then—began Dombey ! "

I know of only one occasion on which he employed an amanuensis, and my aunt is my authority for the following, concerning this one time: " The book which your father dictated to me was 'The Child's History of England.' The reason for my being used in this capacity of secretary was that

'Bleak House' was being written at the
same time, and your father would dictate
to me while walking about the room, as a
relief after his long, sedentary imprison-
ment. The history was being written for
'Household Words,' ,and 'Bleak House'
also as a serial, so he had both weekly and
monthly work on hand at the same time."
The history was dedicated: "To my own
dear children, whom I hope it will help, by-
and-by, to read with interest larger and
better books upon the same subject."

My father wrote always with a quill pen
and blue ink, and never, I think, used a
lead pencil. His handwriting was considered extremely difficult to read by many
people, but I never found it so. In his
manuscripts there were so many erasures,
and such frequent interlineations that a
special staff of compositors was used for his
work, but this was not on account of
any illegibility in his handwriting. The
manuscripts are most of them, exhibited at

the South Kensington Museum in "the
Forster Collection," and they all show I
think, the extreme care and fastidiousness of
the writer, and his ever-constant desire to
improve upon and simplify his original
sentence. His objection to the use of a
lead pencil was so great that even his
personal memoranda, such as his lists of
guests for dinner parties, the arrangement
of tables and menus, were always written
in ink. For his personal correspondence
he used blue note paper, and signed his
name in the left-hand corner of the
envelope. After a morning's close work he
was sometimes quite pre-occupied when he
came into luncheon. Often, when we were
only our home party at "Gad's Hill," he
would come in, take something to eat in a
mechanical way—he never ate but a small
luncheon—and would return to his study to
finish the work he had left, scarcely having
spoken a word in all this time. Again, he
would come in, having finished his work,

but looking very tired and worn. Our talking at these times did not seem to disturb him, though any sudden sound, as the dropping of a spoon, or the clinking of a glass, would send a spasm of pain across his face.

The sudden, almost instantaneous, popularity of "Pickwick" was known to the world long before it was realized by its anxious young author. All the business transactions concerning its publication were modest to a degree, and the preparations for such a success as came to it were none. As to its popularity, Mr. Forster writes: "Judges on the bench, and boys in the streets, gravity and folly, the young and the old, those who were entering life, and those who were quitting it, alike found it irresistible." Carlyle wrote: "An archdeacon repeated to me, with his own venerable lips, the other evening, a strange, profane story of a solemn clergyman who had been summoned to administer consola-

E

tion to a very ill man. As he left the
room he heard the sick man ejaculate: "Well,
thank God, Pickwick will be out in ten
days, anyway!" No young author ever
sprang into more sudden and brilliant
fame than "Boz," and none could have
remained more thoroughly unspoiled, or so
devoid of egotism under success. His own
opinion of his fame, and his estimate of its
value, may be quoted here: "To be
numbered amongst the household gods of
one's distant countrymen, and associated
with their homes and quiet pleasures; to
be told that in each nook and corner of
the world's great mass there lives one
well-wisher who holds communion with
one in the spirit, is a worthy fame, indeed.
That I may be happy enough to cheer
some of your leisure hours for a long time
to come, and to hold a place in your
pleasant thoughts, is the earnest wish of
'Boz.'"

On the Christmas Eve of 1863 my

father was greatly shocked and distressed to hear of the sudden death of Mr. Thackeray. Our guests, naturally, were full of the sad news, and there was a gloom cast over everything. We all thought of the sorrow of his two daughters, who were so devoted to him, and whom his sudden taking away would leave so desolate. In "The Cornhill Magazine" of the February following, my father wrote: "I saw Mr. Thackeray for the first time nearly twenty-eight years ago, when he proposed to become the illustrator of my earliest book. I saw him last shortly before Christmas, at the Athenæum Club, when he told me he had been in bed three days, and that he had it in his mind to try a new remedy, which he laughingly described. He was cheerful, and looked very bright. In the night of that day week he died. * * * * No one can be surer than I of the greatness and goodness of his heart. In no place should I take it upon myself

at this time to discourse of his books, of
his refined knowledge of character, of his
subtle acquaintance with the weakness of
human nature, of his delightful playful-
ness as an essayist, of his quaint and touching ballads, of his mastery over the English
language. But before me lies all that he
had written of his latest story, and the
pain I have felt in perusing it has not been
deeper than the conviction that he was in
the healthiest region of his powers when he
worked on this last labor. The last words
he corrected in print were 'and my heart
throbbed with an exquisite bliss.' God
grant that on that Christmas Eve, when he
laid his head back on his pillow and threw
up his arms as he had been wont to do when
very weary, some consciousness of duty done,
and of Christian hope throughout life humbly
cherished, may have caused his own heart
so to throb when he passed away to his rest."

CHAPTER IV.

Fondness for Athletic Sports.—His love of bathing.—
His study of the raven.—Calling the doctor in.—My father
with our dogs.—The cats of "Gad's Hill."—"Bumble"
and "Mrs. Bouncer."—A strange friendship.

As a child my father was prevented from
any active participation in the sports and
amusements of his boyish companions by
his extreme delicacy and frequent illnesses,
so that until his manhood his knowledge of
games was gained merely from long hours of
watching others while lying upon the grass.
With manhood, however, came the strength
and activity which enabled him to take part
in all kinds of outdoor exercise and sports,
and it seemed that in his passionate enjoyment and participation in those later years
he was recompensed for the weary childhood
years of suffering and inability. Athletic
sports were a passion with him in his manhood, as I have said. In 1839 he rented a

cottage at Petersham, not far from London, "where," to quote from Mr. Forster, "the extensive garden grounds admitted of much athletic competition, in which Dickens, for the most part, held his own against even such accomplished athletes as Maclise and Mr. Beard. Bar leaping, bowling and quoits were among the games carried on with the greatest ardor, and in sustained energy Dickens certainly distanced every competitor. Even the lighter recreations of battledore and bagatelle were pursued with relentless activity. At such amusements as the Petersham races, in those days rather celebrated, and which he visited daily while they lasted, he worked much harder than the running horses did."

Riding was a favorite recreation at all times with my father, and he was constantly inviting one or another of his friends to bear him company on these excursions. Always fond, in his leisure hours, of companions, he seemed to find his rides and walks quite incomplete if made alone, He writes on one occasion : "What think you of a fifteen-mile ride out, ditto in, and a lunch on the road, with a wind-up of six o'clock dinner in Doughty Street?" And again: "Not knowing whether my head was off or on, it became so addled with work, I have gone riding over the old road, and shall be truly delighted to meet or be overtaken by you." As a young man he was extremely fond of riding, but as I never remember seeing him on horseback I think he must have deprived himself of this pastime soon after his marriage.

But walking was, perhaps, his chiefest pleasure, and the country lanes and city streets alike found him a close observer of their beauties and interests. He was a rapid walker, his usual pace being four miles an hour, and to keep step with him required energy and activity similar to his own. In many of his letters he speaks with most evident enjoyment of this pastime. In one he writes : " What a brilliant morning for a country walk ! I start precisely—precisely, mind—at half-past one. Come, come, come and walk in the green lanes ! " Again : " You don't feel disposed, do you, to muffle yourself up and start off with me for a good, brisk walk over Hampstead Heath ? "

Outdoor games of the simpler kinds delighted him. Battledore and shuttlecock was played constantly in the garden at Devonshire Terrace, though I do not remember my father ever playing it elsewhere. The American game of bowls pleased him, and rounders found him more than expert. Croquet he disliked, but cricket he enjoyed intensely as a spectator, always keeping one of the scores during the matches at " Gad's Hill."

He· was a firm believer in the hygiene of bathing, and cold baths, sea baths and shower baths were among his most constant practices. In those days scientific ablution was not very generally practised, and I am

sure that in many places during his travels
my father was looked upon as an amiable
maniac with a penchant for washing.

During his first visit to America, while he
was making some journey in a rather rough
and uncomfortable canal boat, he wrote:
"I am considered very hardy in the morning, for I run up barenecked and plunge my
head into the half-frozen water by half-past
five o'clock.   I am respected for my activity,
inasmuch as I jump from the boat to the
towing path, and walk five or six miles before
breakfast, keeping up with the horses all the
time." And from Broadstairs : "In a bay
window sits, from nine o'clock to one, a
gentleman with rather long hair and no neck-
cloth, who writes and grins as if he thought
he were very funny, indeed.   At one o'clock
he disappears, presently emerges from a
bathing machine, and may be seen a kind of
salmon-colored porpoise, splashing about in
the ocean.   After that, he may be viewed in
another bay window on the ground floor, eat-

ing a good lunch; and after that, walking a dozen miles or so, or lying on his back on the sand reading. Nobody bothers him, unless they know he is disposed to be talked to; and I am told he is very comfortable, indeed."

During the hottest summer months of our year's residence in Italy, we lived at a little seaport of the Mediterranean called Albaro. The bathing here was of the most primitive kind, one division of the clear, dark-blue pools among the rocks being reserved for women, the other for men, and as we children were as much at home in the water as any known variety of fish, we used to look with wonder at the so-called bathing of the Italian women. They would come in swarms, beautifully dressed, and with most elaborately arranged heads of hair, but the slightest of wettings with them was the equivalent of a bath. In the open bay at Albaro the current was very strong, and the bathing most dangerous to even an ex-

perienced swimmer. I remember one morning the terrible fright we were given by an
uncle of ours; he swam out into the bay,
was caught by the current of an ebb tide and
borne out of reach of our eyes. A fishing
boat picked him up still alive, though greatly
exhausted. "It was a world of horror and
anguish crowded into four or five minutes of
dreadful agitation," wrote my father, "and
to complete the terror of it the entire family,
including the children, were on the rock in
full view of it all, crying like mad creatures."

He loved animals, flowers and birds, his
fondness for the latter being shown nowhere
more strongly than in his devotion to his
ravens at Devonshire Terrace. He writes
characteristically of the death of "Grip,"
the first raven : "You will be greatly shocked
and grieved to hear that the raven is no
more. He expired to-day at a few minutes
after twelve o'clock, at noon. He had been
ailing for a few days, but we anticipated no
serious result, conjecturing that a portion of

the white paint he swallowed last summer
might be lingering about his vitals. Yesterday afternoon he was taken so much worse
that I sent an express for the medical gentleman, who promptly attended and administered
a powerful dose of castor oil. Under the
influence of this medicine he recovered so
far as to be able, at eight o'clock, p.m., to
bite Topping (the coachman). His night
was peaceful. This morning, at daybreak,
he appeared better, and partook plentifully
of some warm gruel, the flavor of which he
appeared to relish. Toward eleven o'clock
he was so much worse that it was found
necessary to muffle the stable knocker. At
half-past, or thereabouts, he was heard talking to himself about the horse and Topping's
family, and to add some incoherent expressions which are supposed to have been
either a foreboding of his approaching dis-
solution or some wishes relative to the
disposal of his little property, consisting
chiefly of half-pence which he had buried in

different parts of the garden. On the clock striking twelve he appeared slightly agitated, but he soon recovered, walked twice or thrice along the coach house, stopped to bark, staggered, and exclaimed ' Halloa, old girl !' (his favorite expression) and died. He behaved throughout with decent fortitude, equanimity and self-possession. I deeply regret that, being in ignorance of his danger, I did not attend to receive his last instructions.

"Something remarkable about his eyes occasioned Topping to run for the doctor at twelve. When they returned together, our friend was gone. It was the medical gentleman who informed me of his decease. He did it with caution and delicacy, preparing me by the remark that 'a jolly queer start had taken place.' I am not wholly free from suspicions of poison. A malicious butcher has been heard to say that he would ' do ' for him. His plea was that he would not be molested in taking orders down the mews by any bird that wore a tail. Were they ravens who took manna to somebody in the wilderness? At times I hope they were, and at others I fear they were not, or they would certainly have stolen it by the way. Kate is as well as can be expected. The children seem rather glad of it. He bit their ankles, but that was in play." As my father was writing " Barnaby Rudge" at this time, and wished to continue his study of raven nature, another and a larger " Grip" took the place of "our friend" but it was he whose talking tricks and comical ways gave my father the idea of making a raven one of the characters in this book. My father's fondness for " Grip" was, however, never transferred to any other raven, and none of us ever forgave the butcher whom we all held in some way responsible for his untimely taking off.

But I think his strongest love, among animals, was for dogs. I find a delightful anecdote told by him of a dog belonging to a lady whom he knew well, " Of," an immense, black, good-humored, Newfoundland dog. He came from Oxford and had lived all his life in a brewery. Instructions were given with him that if he were let out every morning alone he would immediately find out the river, regularly take a swim and come gravely home again. This he did with the greatest punctuality, but after a little while was observed to smell of beer. His owner was so sure that he smelled of beer that she resolved to watch him. He was seen to come back from his swim round the usual corner and to go up a flight of steps into a beer shop. Being instantly followed, the beer shopkeeper is seen to take down a pot (pewter pot) and is heard to say: " Well, old chap, come for your beer as usual, have you ? " Upon which he draws a pint and puts it down and the dog drinks it. Being required to explain how this comes to pass the man says: " Yes, ma'am. I know he's your dog, ma'am, but I didn't when he first

came. He looked in, ma'am, as a brickmaker might, and then he come in, as a
brickmaker might, and he wagged his tail
at the pots, and he giv a sniff round and con-
veyed to me as he was used to beer. So I
draw'd him a drop, and he drunk it up.
Next morning he come agen by the clock and
I draw'd him a pint, and ever since he has
took his pint reg'lar."

On account of our birds, cats were not
allowed in the house; but from a friend in
London I received a present of a white
kitten—Williamina—and she and her
numerous offspring had a happy home at
" Gad's Hill." She became a favorite with
all the household, and showed particular
devotion to my father. I remember on one
occasion when she had presented us with a
family of kittens, she selected a corner of
father's study for their home. She brought
them one by one from the kitchen and
deposited them in her chosen corner. My
father called to me to remove them, saying

that he could not allow the kittens to remain in his room. I did so, but Williamina brought them back again, one by one. Again they were removed. The third time, instead of putting them in the corner, she placed them all, and herself beside them, at my father's feet, and gave him such an imploring glance that he could resist no longer, and they were allowed to remain. As the kittens grew older they became more and more frolicsome, swarming up the curtains, playing about on the writing table and scampering behind the book shelves. But they were never complained of and lived happily in the study until the time came for finding them other homes. One of these kittens was kept, who, as he was quite deaf, was left unnamed, and became known by the servants as " the master's cat," because of his devotion to my father. He was always with him, and used to follow him about the garden like a dog, and sit with him while he wrote. One evening we were

F

all, except father, going to a ball, and when
we started, left " the master " and his cat in
the drawing-room together.   " The master "
was reading at a small table, on which a
lighted candle was placed.   Suddenly the
candle went out.   My father, who was much
interested in his book, relighted the candle,
stroked the cat, who was looking at him
pathetically he noticed, and continued his
reading.   A few minutes later, as the light
became dim, he looked up just in time to see
puss deliberately put out the candle with his
paw, and then look appealingly toward him.
This second and unmistakable hint was not
disregarded, and puss was given the petting
he craved.   Father was full of this anecdote
when all met at breakfast the next morning.

Among our dogs were " Turk " and
" Linda," the former a beautiful mastiff and
the latter a soft-eyed, gentle, good-tempered
St. Bernard. " Mrs. Bouncer," a Pomeranian,
came next, a tiny ball of white fluffy fur, who
came as a special gift to me, and speedily

won her way by her grace and daintiness
into the affections of every member of the
household. My father became her special
slave, and had a peculiar voice for her—as
he had for us, when we were children—to
which she would respond at once by running
to him from any part of the house when she
heard his call. He delighted to see her with
the large dogs, with whom she gave herself
great airs, " because," as he said, " she looks
so preposterously small." A few years later
came " Don," a Newfoundland, and then
" Bumble," his son, named after " Oliver
Twist's " beadle, because of " a peculiarly
pompous and overbearing manner he had of
appearing to mount guard over the yard
when he was an absolute infant." Lastly
came " Sultan," an Irish bloodhound, who
had a bitter experience with his life at
" Gad's Hill." One evening, having broken
his chain, he fell upon a little girl who was
passing and bit her so severely that my father
considered it necessary to have him shot,

although this decision cost him a great deal of sorrow.

For a short time I had the care of a mongrel called " Gipsy." She was not allowed to enter any of the family rooms, and used to spend her time lying contentedly on the rug outside the drawing-room. One afternoon a friend came from Chatham bringing with him a wonderful poodle who had been specially invited to perform all his tricks for my father's enjoyment. On his arrival, " Mrs. Bouncer " became furious, and when he began his tricks she went deliberately into the hall and escorted " Gipsy " into the drawing-room, as much as to say: " I can't stand this. If strange dogs are to be made much of, surely the dogs in the house may be at least permitted to enter the room." She would not look at " Fosco," the poodle, but sat throughout his performance with her back toward him, the picture of offended dignity. Just as soon, however, as he was fairly out of the house, and not until then, she escorted "Gipsy" back to her rug. My father was intensely amused by this behaviour of "Bouncer's" and delighted in telling this story about her.

"Mrs. Bouncer" was honored by many messages from her master during his absences from home. Here is one written as I was convalescing from a serious illness: "In my mind's eye I behold 'Mrs. Bouncer,' still with some traces of anxiety on her faithful countenance, balancing herself a little unequally on her forelegs, pricking up her ears with her head on one side, and slightly opening her intellectual nostrils. I send my loving and respectful duty to her." Again: "Think of my dreaming of 'Mrs. Bouncer,' each night !!!"

My father's love for dogs led him into a strange friendship during our stay at Boulogne. There lived in a cottage on the street which led from our house to the town, a cobbler who used to sit at his window working all day with his dog—a Pomeranian

—on the table beside him. The cobbler, in whom my father became very much interested because of the intelligence of his Pomeranian companion, was taken ill, and for many months was unable to work. My father writes : " The cobbler has been ill these many months. The little dog sits at the door so unhappy and anxious to help that I every day expect to see him beginning a pair of top boots." Another time father writes in telling the history of this little animal : " A cobbler at Boulogne, who had the nicest of little dogs that always sat in his sunny window watching him at his work, asked me if I would bring the dog home as he couldn't afford to pay the tax for him. The cobbler and the dog being both my particular friends I complied. The cobbler parted with the dog heartbroken. When the dog got home here, my man, like an idiot as he is, tied him up and then untied him. The moment the gate was open, the dog (on the very day after his arrival) ran out. Next day Georgy and I saw him lying

MRS. BOUNCER.

MISS DICKENS POMERANIAN,

"MRS. BOUNCER."

URRY, lazy, warm and bright,
Peeping from her fringe of white,
She blinks and sleeps both day and night,

   A happy Spitz!

She need not fear the cruel stick,
Nor has she learnt a single trick—
Just deigns her mistress' hand to lick,

   As she knits.

She eats, and drinks, and eats again,
Is never out in wind or rain,—
Takes many a journey in the train,

   That lucky Spitz!

The guard for other dogs has knocks—
For *her* ne'er points to gloomy box
But courteously the door unlocks,

   And her admits.

She has her own coquettish charms,
Knows no sorrows, no alarms,
And dozes in her mistress' arms—

   A sleepy Spitz.

How small and piquant are her feet—
Ben Allen's sister had as neat—
She looks so saucy, one could beat

   Her into fits.

Quite ravishing when neat and clean,
Her ears seem lined with ermoline
She rules the house, a haughty queen,

   A saucy Spitz!

Just tolerates the frequent hug—
Snoozing all day upon the rug,
Complacent, philosophic—snug,

   Her paws like mits

At dinner—ah! that pleasant Babel!
Touch her paw beneath the table,
She'd bite your foot—were she but able—

   A naughty Spitz.

To find her mistress how she flew!
Faithful the coming step she knew
Let others be as brave and true—

   Lords or Wits!

When SULTAN, TURK, and LINDA fleet
The lost lov'd Master rushed to meet,
His kindly voice would always greet

   The little Spitz!

Alas! so furry, warm, and white,
From this cold world she took her flight,
No more on rug, by fireside bright,

   Dear BOUNCER sits.

  PERCY FitzGerald.

all covered with mud, dead, outside the neighbouring church. How am I ever to tell the cobbler? He is too poor to come to England, so I feel that I must lie to him for life, and say that the dog is fat and happy."

Of horses and ponies we possessed but few during our childhood, and these were not of very choice breed. I remember, however, one pretty pony which was our delight, and dear old " Toby," the good sturdy horse which for many years we used at " Gad's Hill." My father, however, was very fond of horses, and I recall hearing him comment on the strange fact that an animal " so noble in its qualities should be the cause of so much villainy."

CHAPTER V.

The warm affection which was so
characteristic of my father toward people was
also directed, as I have already told, towards
animals and birds. A few further anecdotes
occur to me, and I have ventured to give them
here, before proceeding to tell of his visit to
America, his readings, and the, to me, sad
story of his last public appearance.

My father's quick and amusing observation
of London birds and their habits, and of their
fondness for "low company," is full of charm
and quaint oddity. He writes: "That anything born of an egg and invested with wings
should have got to the pass that it hops contentedly down a ladder into a cellar, and calls
that going home, is a circumstance so amazing

as to leave one nothing more in this connection to wonder at. I know a low fellow,
originally of a good family from Dorking,
who takes his whole establishment of wives
in single file in at the door of the jug depart-
ment of a disorderly tavern near the Hay-
market, manœuvres them among the
company's legs, and emerges with them at the
bottle entrance, seldom in the season going
to bed before two in the morning. And thus
he passes his life. But the family I am best
acquainted with reside in the densest part of
Bethnal Green. Their abstraction from the
objects in which they live, or rather their conviction that these objects have all come into
existence in express subservience to fowls, has
so enchanted me that I have made them the
subject of many journeys at divers hours.
After careful observation of the two lords and
of the ten ladies of whom this family consists,
I have come to the conclusion that their
opinions are represented by the leading lord
and leading lady, the latter, as I judge, an

aged personage, afflicted with a paucity of
feather and visibility of quill that gives her the
appearance of a bundle of office pens. They
look upon old shoes, wrecks of kettles, sauce-
pans and fragments of bonnets as a kind of
meteoric discharge for fowls to peck at.
Gaslight comes quite as natural to them as
any other light ; and I have more than a
suspicion that in the minds of the two lords,
the early public house at the corner has
superseded the sun. They always begin tc
crow when the public house shutters begin to
be taken down, and they salute the pot-boy
the instant he appears to perform that duty,
as if he were Phœbus in person."

During one of his walks through the slums,
my father was so fascinated by the intelligence
of a busy goldfinch drawing water for himself
in his cage—he had other accomplishments as
well—that he went in and bought it. But
not a thing would the little bird do, not a
trick would he perform when he got to his
new home in Doughty Street, and would only

draw up water in the dark or when he thought no one was looking. "After an interval of futile and at length hopeless expectation," my father writes, " the merchant who had educated him was appealed to. The merchant was a bow-legged character, with a flat and cushiony nose, like the last new strawberry. He wore a fur cap and shorts, and was of the velveteen race velveteeny. He sent word that he would ' look round.' He looked round, appeared in the doorway of the room, and slightly cocked up his evil eye at the goldfinch. Instantly a raging thirst beset the bird, and when it was appeased he still drew several unnecessary buckets of water, leaping about the perch and sharpening his bill with irrepressible satisfaction."

While at Broadstairs one summer, our bathing woman, who reared birds, gave a canary to my sister and myself. "Dick," who was only a few weeks old when he came to us, grew to be a very king of birds, and became in time a most important member of the house-

hold. There was a fierce war waged against
cats during his lifetime, and writing from
Boulogne my father very funnily describes
our troubles with the feline race: "War is
raging against two particularly tigerish and
fearful cats (from the mill, I suppose), which
are always glaring in dark corners after our
wonderful little ' Dick.' Keeping the house
open at all points it is impossible to shut them
out, and they hide themselves in the most
terrific manner, hanging themselves up behind
draperies like bats, and tumbling out in the
dead of night with frightful caterwaulings.
Hereupon French, the footman, borrows a gun,
loads it to the muzzle, discharges it twice in
vain, and throws himself over with the recoil
exactly like a clown. But at last, while I was
in town, he aims at the more amiable cat of
the two and shoots that animal dead.
Insufferably elated by this victory he is now
engaged from morning to night in hiding
behind bushes to get aim at the other. He
does nothing else whatever. All the boys

encourage him and watch for the enemy, on whose appearance they give an alarm, which immediately serves as a warning to the creature, who runs away.   They—the boys—are at this moment (ready dressed for church) all lying on their stomachs in various parts of the garden.   I am afraid to go out lest I should be shot.   Mr. Plornish, says his prayers at night in a whisper lest the cat should overhear him and take offence.   The tradesmen cry out as they come up the avenue : ' *Me Voici ! C'est Moi—boulanger— me tirez pas, Monsieur Frenche !* '   It is like living in a state of siege, and the wonderful manner in which the cat preserves the character of being the only person not much put out by the intensity of this monomania is most ridiculous.   The finest thing is that immediately after I have heard the noble sportsman blazing away at her in the garden in front I look out of my room door into the drawing-room and am pretty sure to see her coming in after the bird, in the calmest

manner possible, by the back window." But
no harm ever came to " our wonderful little
' Dick,' " who lived to a ripe old age—sixteen
years—and was buried under a rose tree at
" Gad's Hill."

On his return from his last visit to America
he wrote a charming account of his welcome
home by the dogs at " Gad's Hill." " As you
ask me about the dogs, I begin with them.
When I came down first I came to Gravesend,
five miles off. The two Newfoundland dogs
coming to meet me with the usual carriage
and the usual driver, and beholding me coming in my usual dress out at the usual door,
it struck me that their recollection of my
having been absent for any unusual time was
at once cancelled. They behaved (they are
both young dogs) exactly in their usual
manner, coming behind the basket phaeton as
we trotted along and lifting their heads to
have their ears pulled, a special attention
which they received from no one else. But
when I drove into the stableyard, ' Linda ' was

greatly excited ; weeping profusely, and throwing herself on her back that she might caress
my foot with her great forepaws. Mamie's
little dog, too, ' Mrs. Bouncer,' barked in the
greatest agitation on being called down and
asked : ' Who is this ?,' tore round me, like the
dog in the Faust outlines."

My father brought with him, on his return
from his first visit to America, a small, shaggy
Havana spaniel, which had been given to him
and which he had named " Timber Doodle."
He wrote of him : " Little doggy improves
rapidly and now jumps over my stick at the
word of command." " Timber," travelled with
us in all our foreign wanderings, and while at
Albaro the poor little fellow had a most unfortunate experience—an encounter of some
duration with a plague of fleas. Father
writes : " ' Timber' has had every hair upon
his body cut off because of the fleas, and he
looks like the ghost of a drowned dog come
out of a pond after a week or so. It is very
awful to see him sidle into a room He knows

the change upon him, and is always turning
round and round to look for himself.   I think
he'll die of grief; it is to be hoped that the
hair will grow again."

For many years my father's public readings
were an important part of his life, and into
their performance and preparation he threw
the best energy of his heart and soul, practising and rehearsing at all times and places.
The meadow near our home was a favorite
place, and people passing through the lane,
not knowing who he was, or what doing,
must have thought him a madman from his
reciting and gesticulation.   The great success
of these readings led to many tempting offers
from the United States, which, as time went
on, and we realized how much the fatigue of
the readings together with his other work
were sapping his strength, we earnestly
opposed his even considering.   However,
after much discussion and deliberation he
wrote to me on September 28th, 1867:   "As I
telegraphed after I saw you I am off to con-

sult with Mr. Forster and Dolby together.
You shall hear either on Monday or by Monday's post from London how I decide finally."
Three days later: "You will have had my
telegram that I go to America. After a long
discussion with Forster and consideration of
what is to be said on both sides, I have
decided to go through with it, and have telegraphed 'yes' to Boston." There was, at
first, some talk of my accompanying him, but
when the programme of the tour was submitted to my father and he saw how much
time must be devoted to business and how
little, indeed almost no time could be given
to sightseeing, this idea was given up.

A farewell banquet was given him in
London on the second of November, and on
the ninth he sailed. A large party of us went
to Liverpool to see him sail, and with heavy
hearts to bid him farewell. In those days a
journey to America was a serious matter, and
we felt in our hearts that he was about to tax

G

his health and strength too cruelly. And so
he did.

Soon after reaching the United States, my
father contracted a severe cold which never
left him during his visit, and which caused
him the greatest annoyance.   I will give you
a few quotations from his letters to show how
pluckily he fought against his ailment and
under what a strain he continued his work.
On his arrival at New York on Christmas Day,
in response to a letter of mine which awaited
him there, he wrote : " I wanted your letter
much, for I had a frightful cold (English colds
are nothing to those of this country) and was
very miserable." He adds to this letter, a day
or two later : " I managed to read last night
but it was as much as I could do. To-day I
am so unwell that I have sent for a doctor."
Again he writes : " It likewise happens, not
seldom, that I am so dead beat when I come
off the stage, that they lay me down on a sofa
after I have been washed and dressed, and I
lie there extremely faint for a quarter of an

hour.   In that time I rally and come right."
Again : " On the afternoon of my birthday my
catarrh was in such a state that Charles
Sumner coming in at five o'clock and finding
me covered with mustard poultices and apparently voiceless, turned to Dolby and said :
'Surely, Mr. Dolby, it is impossible that he
can read to-night.'   Says Dolby : 'Sir, I have
told Mr. Dickens so four times to-day and I
have been very anxious.   But you have no
idea how he will change when he gets to the
little table.'   After five minutes of the little
table I was not, for the time, even hoarse.
The frequent experience of this return of
force when it is wanted saves me much
anxiety, but I am not at times without the
nervous dread that I may some day sink
altogether."

But as a reward for his unstinted self-giving
came the wonderful success of his tour, the
pride and delight which he felt in the
enthusiasm which greeted him everywhere,
the personal affection lavished upon him, and

the many dear friends he made. He writes
from Boston, *à propos* of these rewards:
" When we reached here last Saturday night
we found that Mrs. Fields had not only
garnished the room with flowers, but also with
holly (with real red berries), and festoons of
moss dependent from the looking-glasses and
picture-frames. The homely Christmas look
of the place quite affected us."

Later, from Washington : " I couldn't help
laughing at myself on my birthday here ; it
was observed as much as though I were a little
boy. Flowers and garlands of the most
exquisite kind, arranged in all manner of
green baskets, bloomed over the room ; letters,
radiant with good wishes, poured in. Also,
by hands unknown, the hall at night was
decorated ; and after ' Boots at the Holly
Tree Inn ' the audience rose, great people and
all, standing and cheering until I went back
to the table and made them a little speech."

He wrote home constantly, giving frequent
commissions for improvements at " Gad's

THE EMPTY CHAIR.

Hill," to be made before his return. He was much impressed on his second visit, as on his first, I remember, with the beauty of the American women. "The ladies are remarkably handsome," he wrote.

In the autumn of 1869 he began a series of farewell readings, which were another heavy tax upon his health and strength. During his tour at this time he writes to Mr. Forster after some rather alarming symptoms had developed : " I told Beard, a year after the Staplehurst accident, that I was certain that my heart had been fluttered and wanted a little helping. This the stethoscope confirmed ; and considering the immense exertion I am undergoing, and the constant jarring of express trains, the case seems to me quite intelligible. Don't say anything in the ' Gad's ' direction about my being a little out of sorts. I have broached the matter, of course, but very lightly."

But even such warning as this failed to make him realize how much less was his strength, and with indomitable courage and spirit he continued his tour. The trouble in his feet increased, and his sufferings from this cause were very great. It became necessary at one time for him to have a physician in attendance upon him at every reading. But in spite of his perseverance, he became so ill that the readings had to be stopped.

CHAPTER VI.

Last words spoken in public.—A railroad accident in
1865.—At home after his American visit.—"Improvements" at "Gad's Hill."—At "Gad's Hill" once more.
—The closing days of his life.—Burial at Westminster.

My father gave his last reading in St.
James' Hall, London, on the fifteenth of
March. The programme included "The
Christmas Carol" and the "Trial" from
"Pickwick." The hall was packed by an
enormous audience, and he was greeted with
all the warmth which the personal affection
felt for the reader inspired. We all felt very
anxious for him, fearing that the excitement
and emotion which must attend upon his
public farewell would have a bad effect upon
him. But it had no immediate result, at any
rate, much to our relief.

I do not think that my father ever—and
this is saying a great deal—looked hand-

somer nor read with more ability than on this, his last appearance. Mr. Forster writes: " The charm of his reading was at its height when he shut the volume of 'Pickwick' and spoke in his own person. He said that for fifteen years he had been reading his own books to audiences whose sensitive and kindly recognition of them had given him instruction and enjoyment in his art such as few men could have had ; but that he nevertheless thought it well now to retire upon older associations, and in future to devote himself exclusively to the calling which first made him known. 'In but two short weeks from this time I hope that you may enter in your own homes on a new series of readings, at which my assistance will be indispensable ; but from these garish lights I vanish now, for evermore, with a heartfelt, grateful, respectful, affectionate farewell.' "

There was a dead silence as my father turned away, much moved ; and then came from the audience such a burst and tumult

of cheers and applause as were almost too
much to bear, mixed as they were with
personal love and affection for the man
before them. He returned with us all to
" Gad's Hill," very happy and hopeful,
under the temporary improvement which the
rest and peace of his home brought him,
and he settled down to his new book,
" Edwin Drood," with increased pleasure and
interest.

His last public appearances were in April.
On the fifth he took the chair at the News-
venders' dinner. On the thirtieth he returned
thanks for " Literature" at the Royal
Academy banquet. In this speech he
alluded to the death of his old friend, Mr.
Daniel Maclise, winding up thus: " No
artist, of whatsoever denomination, I make
bold to say, ever went to his rest leaving a
golden memory more pure from dross, or
having devoted himself with a truer chivalry
to the art-goddess whom he worshipped."
These words, with the old, true, affectionate

ring in them, were the last spoken by my father in public.

About 1865 my dear father's health began to give way, a peculiar affection of the foot, which frequently caused him the greatest agony and suffering, appearing about this time. Its real cause—overwork—was not suspected either by his physicians or himself, his vitality seeming something which could not wear out; but, although he was so active and full of energy, he was never really strong, and found soon that he must take more in the way of genuine recreation. He wrote me from France about this time: " Before I went away I had certainly worked myself into a damaged state. But the moment I got away I began, thank God, to get well. I hope to profit from this experience, and to make future dashes from my desk before I need them."

It was while on his way home after this trip that he was in the terrible railroad accident to which he afterwards referred in a

letter to a friend, saying, that his heart had
never been in good condition after that
accident. It occurred on the ninth of June,
a date which five years later was the day
of his death.

He wrote describing his experiences: "I
was in the only carriage which did not go
over into the stream. It was caught upon
the turn by some of the ruin of the bridge,
and became suspended and balanced in
an apparently impossible manner. Two
ladies were my fellow-passengers, an old one
and a young one. This is exactly what
passed—you may judge from it the length
of our suspense: Suddenly we were off the
rail and beating the ground as the car of a
half-emptied balloon might. The old lady
cried out 'My God!' and the young one
screamed. I caught hold of them both (the
old lady sat opposite, and the young one on
my left) and said: 'We can't help ourselves, but we can be quiet and composed.
Pray, don't cry out!' The old lady im-

mediately answered: 'Thank you, rely
upon me. Upon my soul I will be quiet.'
We were then all tilted down together in a
corner of the carriage, which then stopped.
I said to them thereupon: 'You may be
sure nothing worse can happen; our danger
must be over. Will you remain here without stirring while I get out of the window?'
They both answered quite collectedly 'Yes,'
and I got out without the least notion of
what had happened. Fortunately I got out
with great caution, and stood upon the step.
Looking down I saw the bridge gone, and
nothing below me but the line of rail.
Some people in the other two compartments
were madly trying to plunge out at a
window, and had no idea that there was an
open, swampy field fifteen feet down below
them, and nothing else. The two guards
(one with his face cut) were running up and
down on the down-track of the bridge (which
was not torn up) quite wildly. I called out
to them: 'Look at me! Do stop an in-

stant and look at me, and tell me whether
you don't know me?' One of them answered: 'We know you very well, Mr. Dickens.'
'Then,' I said, 'my good fellow, for God's
sake, give me your key, and send one of
those laborers here, and I'll empty this
carriage.' We did it quite safely, by means
of a plank or two, and when it was done I
saw all the rest of the train, except the two
baggage vans, down the stream. I got into
the carriage again for my brandy flask, took
off my travelling hat for a basin, climbed
down the brickwork, and filled my hat with
water. Suddenly I came upon a staggering
man, covered with blood (I think he must
have been flung clean out of his carriage),
with such a frightful cut across the skull
that I couldn't bear to look at him. I
poured some water over his face, and gave
him some to drink, then gave him some
brandy, and laid him down on the grass.

He said 'I am gone,' and died afterwards.
Then I stumbled over a lady lying on her

back against a little pollard tree, with the blood streaming over her face (which was lead color) in a number of distinct little streams from the head. I asked her if she could swallow a little brandy, and she just nodded, and I gave her some and left her for somebody else. The next time I passed her she was dead. Then a man examined at the inquest yesterday (who evidently had not the least remembrance of what really passed) came running up to me and implored me to help him find his wife, who was afterward found dead. No imagination can conceive the ruin of the carriages, or the extraordinary weights under which the people were lying, or the complications into which they were twisted up among iron and wood, and mud and water. I am keeping very quiet here."

This letter was written from "Gad's Hill" four days after the accident. We were spared any anxiety about our father, as we did not hear of the accident until after we were with

him in London. With his usual care and
thoughtfulness he had telegraphed to his
friend Mr. Wills, to summon us to town to
meet him. The letter continues: "I have,
I don't know what to call it, constitutional
(I suppose) presence of mind, and was not
the least fluttered at the time. I instantly
remembered that I had the MS. of a number
with me, and clambered back into the
carriage for it. But in writing these scanty
words of recollection I feel the shake, and
am obliged to stop."

We heard, afterwards, how helpful he had
been at the time, ministering to the dying!
How calmly and tenderly he cared for the
suffering ones about him!

But he never recovered entirely from the
shock. More than a year later he writes:
"It is remarkable that my watch (a special
chronometer) has never gone quite correctly
since, and to this day there sometimes comes
over me, on a railway and in a hansom-cab,
or any sort of conveyance, for a few seconds,

a vague sense of dread that I have no power
to check. It comes and passes, but I
cannot prevent its coming."

I have often seen this dread come upon
him, and on one occasion, which I especially
recall, while we were on our way from
London to our little country station
"Higham," where the carriage was to meet
us, my father suddenly clutched the arms
of the railway carriage seat, while his face
grew ashy pale, and great drops of perspira-
tion stood upon his forehead, and though
he tried hard to master the dread, it was so
strong that he had to leave the train at the
next station. The accident had left its
impression upon the memory, and it was
destined never to be effaced. The hours
spent upon railroads were thereafter often
hours of pain to him. I realized this often
while travelling with him, and no amount of
assurance could dispel the feeling.

Early in May of 1868, we had him safely
back with us, greatly strengthened and in-

vigorated by his ocean journey home, and I think he was never happier at "Gad's Hill" than during his last two years there.

During that time he had a succession of guests, and none were more honored, nor more heartily welcomed, than his American friends. The first of these to come, If I remember rightly, was Mr. Longfellow, with his daughters. My father writes describing a picnic which he gave them ; "I turned out a couple of postilions in the old red jacket of the old Royal red for our ride, and it was like a holiday ride in England fifty years ago. Of course we went to look at the old houses in Rochester, and the old Cathedral, and the old castle, and the house for the six poor travellers.

"Nothing can surpass the respect paid to Longfellow here, from the Queen downward. He is everywhere received and courted, and finds the working men at least as well acquainted with his books as the classes socially above them."

Between the comings and goings of visitors there were delightfully quiet evenings at home, spent during the summer in our lovely porch, or walking about the garden, until "tray time," ten o'clock. When the cooler nights came we had music in the drawing-room, and it is my happiness now to remember on how many evenings I played and sang all his favorite songs and tunes to my father during these last winters while he would listen while he smoked or read, or, in his more usual fashion, paced up and down the room. I never saw him more peacefully contented than at these times.

There were always "improvements"—as my father used to call his alterations—being made at "Gad's Hill," and each improvement was supposed to be the last. As each was completed, my sister—who was always a constant visitor, and an exceptionally dear one to my father—would have to come down and inspect, and as each was displayed, my father would say to her most solemnly:

"Now, Katie, you behold your parent s latest and last achievement." These "last improvements" became quite a joke between them. I remember so well, on one such occasion, after the walls and doors of the drawing-room had been lined with mirrors, my sister's laughing speech to "the master": "I believe papa, that when you become an angel your wings will be made of looking-glass and your crown of scarlet geraniums."

And here I would like to correct an error concerning myself. I have been spoken of as my father's "favorite daughter." If he had a favorite daughter—and I hope and believe that the one was as dear to him as the other—my dear sister must claim that honor. I say this ungrudgingly, for during those last two years my father and I seemed to become more closely united, and I know how deep was the affectionate intimacy at the time of his death.

The "last improvement"—in truth, the very last—was the building of a conservatory between the drawing and dining rooms. My father was more delighted with this than with any previous alteration, and it was certainly a pretty addition to the quaint old villa. The châlet, too, which he used in summer as his study, was another favorite spot at his favorite "Gad's Hill."

In the early months of 1870 we moved up to London, as my father had decided to give twelve farewell readings there. He had the sanction of the late Sir Thomas Watson to this undertaking, on condition that there should be no railway journeys in connection with them. While we were in London he made many private engagements, principally, I know, on my account, as I was to be presented that spring.

During this last visit to London, my father was not, however, in his usual health, and was so quickly and easily tired that a great number of our engagements had to be cancelled. He dined out very seldom, and I remember that on the last occasion he attended a very large dinner party the effort was too much for him, and before the gentlemen returned to the drawing-room, he sent me a message begging me to come to him at once, saying that he was in too great pain to mount the stairs. No one who had watched him throughout the dinner, seeing his bright, animated face, and listening to his cheery conversation, could have imagined him to be suffering acute pain.

He was at "Gad's Hill" again by the thirtieth of May, and soon hard at work upon "Edwin Drood." Although happy and contented, there was an appearance of fatigue and weariness about him very unlike his usual air of fresh activity. He was out with the dogs for the last time on the afternoon of the sixth of June, when he walked into Rochester for the "Daily Mail." My sister, who had come to see the latest "improvement," was visiting us, and was to take me with her to London on her return, for a short visit. The conservatory—the "improvement" which Katie had been summoned to inspect—had been stocked, and by this time many of the plants were in full blossom. Everything was at its brightest and I remember distinctly my father's pleasure in showing my sister the beauties of his "improvement."

We had been having most lovely weather, and in consequence, the outdoor plants were wonderfully forward in their bloom, my father's favorite red geraniums making a blaze of color in the front garden. The syringa shrubs filled the evening air with sweetest fragrance as we sat in the porch and walked about the garden on this last Sunday of our dear father's life. My aunt and I retired early and my dear sister sat for a long while with my father while he spoke to her most earnestly of his affairs.

As I have already said my father had such an intense dislike for leave-taking that he always, when it was possible, shirked a farewell, and we children, knowing this dislike, used only to wave our hands or give him a silent kiss when parting. But on this

Monday morning, the seventh, just as we were about to start for London, my sister suddenly said : " I *must* say good-bye to papa," and hurried over to the châlet where he was busily writing. As a rule when he was so occupied, my father would hold up his cheek to be kissed, but this day he took my sister in his arms saying : "God bless you, Katie," and there, " among the branches of the trees, among the birds and butterflies and the scent of flowers," she left him, never to look into his eyes again.

In the afternoon, feeling fatigued, and not inclined to much walking, he drove with my aunt into Cobham. There he left the carriage and walked home through the park. After dinner he remained seated in the dining-room, through the evening, as from that room he could see the effect of some lighted Chinese lanterns, which he had hung in the conservatory during the day, and talked to my aunt about his great love for " Gad's Hill," his wish that his name might become more associated with the place, and his desire to be buried near it.

On the morning of the eighth he was in excellent spirits, speaking of his book, at which he intended working through the day, and in which he was most intensely interested. He spent a busy morning in the châlet, and it must have been then that he wrote that description of Rochester, which touched our hearts when we read it for the first time after its writer lay dead : " Brilliant morning shines on the old city. Its antiquities and ruins are surpassingly beautiful with the lusty ivy gleaming in the sun and the rich trees waving in the balmy air. Changes of glorious light from moving boughs, songs of birds, scents from gardens, woods and fields, or rather, from the one great garden of the whole cultivated island in its yielding time, penetrate into the cathedral, subdue its earthly odor, and preach the Resurrection and the Life."

He returned to the house for luncheon,

seemingly perfectly well and exceedingly
cheerful and hopeful. He smoked a cigar
in his beloved conservatory, and went back
to the châlet. When he came again to the
house, about an hour before the time fixed
for an early dinner, he was tired, silent and
abstracted, but as this was a mood very
usual to him after a day of engrossing work,
it caused no alarm nor surprise to my aunt,
who happened to be the only member of
the family at home. While awaiting dinner
he wrote some letters in the library and
arranged some trifling business matters, with
a view to his departure for London the
following morning.

It was not until they were seated at the
dinner-table that a striking change in the
color and expression of his face startled my
aunt. Upon her asking him if he were ill,
he answered "Yes, very ill; I have been
very ill for the last hour." But when she
said that she would send for a physician he

stopped her, saying that he would go on
with dinner, and afterward to London.

He made an earnest effort to struggle
against the seizure which was fast coming
over him, and continued to talk, but in-
coherently and very indistinctly. It being
now evident that he was in a serious condition, my aunt begged him to go to his room
before she sent for medical aid. "Come
and lie down," she entreated. "Yes, on
the ground," he answered indistinctly, These
were the last words that he uttered. As he
spoke, he fell to the floor. A couch was
brought into the dining-room, on which he
was laid, a messenger was dispatched for the
local physician, telegrams were sent to all of
us and to Mr. Beard. This was at a few
minutes after six o'clock. I was dining at a
house some little distance from my sister's
home. Dinner was half over when I received
a message that she wished to speak to me.
I found her in the hall with a change of
dress for me and a cab in waiting. Quickly

I changed my gown, and we began the short journey which brought us to our so sadly-altered home. Our dear aunt was waiting for us at the open door, and when I saw her face I think the last faint hope died within me.

All through the night we watched him— my sister on one side of the couch, my aunt on the other, and I keeping hot bricks to the feet which nothing could warm, hoping and praying that he might open his eyes and look at us, and know us once again. But he never moved, never opened his eyes, never showed a sign of consciousness through all the long night. On the afternoon of the ninth the celebrated London physician, Dr. Russell Reynolds, (recently deceased), was summoned to a consultation by the two medical men in attendance, but he could only confirm their hopeless verdict. Later, in the evening of this day, at ten minutes past six, we saw a shudder pass over our dear father, he heaved a deep sigh, a large tear rolled down his face and at that instant his spirit left us. As we saw the dark shadow pass from his face, leaving it so calm and beautiful in the peace and majesty of death, I think there was not one of us who would have wished, could we have had the power, to recall his spirit to earth.

━━━━━━━━━━━━━

I made it my duty to guard the beloved body as long as it was left to us. The room in which my dear father reposed for the last time was bright with the beautiful fresh flowers which were so abundant at this time of the year, and which our good neighbours sent to us so frequently. The birds were singing all about and the summer sun shone brilliantly.

"And may there be no sadness of farewell
          When I embark.
For though when from out our bourne of Time and Place
          The flood may bear me far,
I hope to see my Pilot face to face
          When I have crossed the bar.'

Those exquisite lines of Lord Tennyson's

seem so appropriate to my father, to his dread of good-byes, to his great and simple faith, that I have ventured to quote them here.

On the morning after he died, we received a very kind visit from Sir John Millais, then Mr. Millais, R.A. and Mr. Woolner, R.A. Sir John made a beautiful pencil drawing of my father, and Mr. Woolner took a cast of his head, from which he afterwards modelled a bust. The drawing belongs to my sister, and is one of her greatest treasures. It is, like all Sir John's drawings, most delicate and refined, and the likeness absolutely faithful to what my father looked in death.

You remember that when he was describing the illustrations of Little Nell's death-bed he wrote: " I want it to express the most beautiful repose and tranquillity, and to have something of a happy look, if death can." Surely this was what his death-bed expressed—infinite happiness and rest.

As my father had expressed a wish to be buried in the quiet little church-yard at Shorne, arrangements were made for the interment to take place there. This intention was, however, abandoned, in consequence of a request from the Dean and chapter of Rochester Cathedral that his bones might repose there. A grave was prepared and everything arranged when it was made known to us, through Dean Stanley, that there was a general and very earnest desire that he should find his last resting-place in Westminster Abbey. To such a tribute to our dear father's memory we could make no possible objection, although it was with great regret that we relinquished the plan to lay him in a spot so closely identified with his life and works.

The only stipulation which was made in connection with the burial at Westminster Abbey was that the clause in his will which read : " I emphatically direct that I be buried in an inexpensive, unostentatious and

CHARLES DICKENS' GRAVE.

and strictly private manner," should be strictly adhered to, as it was.

At midday on the fourteenth of June a few friends and ourselves saw our dear one laid to rest in the grand old cathedral. Our small group in that vast edifice seemed to make the beautiful words of our beautiful burial service even more than usually solemn and touching. Later in the day, and for many following days, hundreds of mourners flocked to the open grave, and filled the deep vault with flowers. And even after it was closed Dean Stanley wrote: "There was a constant pressure to the spot and many flowers were strewn upon it by unknown hands, many tears shed from unknown eyes."

And every year on the ninth of June and on Christmas day we find other flowers strewn by other unknown hands on that spot so sacred to us, as to all who knew and loved him. And every year beautiful bright-coloured leaves are sent to us from across the Atlantic, to be placed with our own flowers on that dear grave; and it is twenty-six years now since my father died!

And for his epitaph what better than my father's own words:

"Of the loved, revered and honoured head, thou canst not turn one hair to thy dread purposes, nor make one feature odious. It is not that the hand is heavy and will fall down when released; it is not that the heart and pulse are still; but that the hand was open, generous and true, the heart brave, warm and tender, and the pulse a man's. Strike! shadow, strike! and see his good deeds springing from the wound, to sow the world with life immortal."

THE END.

EX LIBRIS
ROXBURCHE
PrESS